FIGHTER PLANES

MARK DARTFORD

angus

This edition published in 2004 by Angus Books
12 Ravensbury Terrace
London
SW18 4RL

ISBN 1-904594-34-4

The Brown Reference Group plc
8 Chapel Place
Rivington Street
London
EC2A 3DQ

Production by Omnipress,
Eastbourne, UK
Printed and bound in Dubai

This book uses black and yellow chevrons as a decorative element on some headers. They do not point to other elements on the page.

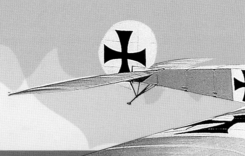

Contents

Introduction

White **vapour trails** twist around the skies as the faint sound of cannon fire reaches the ground. Suddenly, one trail turns to black smoke and spirals down. A combat ends in a kill.

Early Days

From the earliest days, military leaders in several countries took an interest in aviation. Before World War I (1914–1918), aeroplanes were tested for use in aerial observation. The cavalry worried that noise from aircraft engines would alarm the horses.

BALLOON WARFARE

Balloons had been used for aerial observation in the Civil War (1861–1865). Aeroplanes could get around more quickly than balloons and could view enemy positions above the range of artillery.

>> **vapour trail** = a condensation track made by aircraft moving through cold air

World War I

The earliest aeroplanes that flew over the battlefield in World War I were named scouts. They usually carried a pilot and an observer. When enemy scouts first met in the skies, the observers fired rifles at each other. Later aeroplanes were fitted with machine guns in the observer's cockpit.

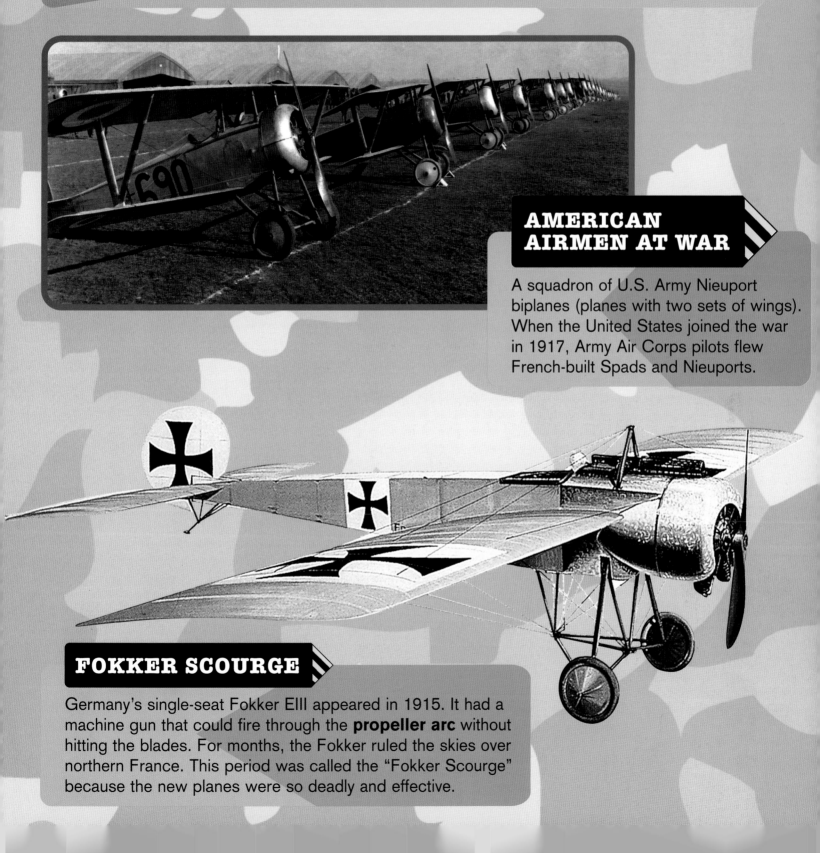

AMERICAN AIRMEN AT WAR

A squadron of U.S. Army Nieuport biplanes (planes with two sets of wings). When the United States joined the war in 1917, Army Air Corps pilots flew French-built Spads and Nieuports.

FOKKER SCOURGE

Germany's single-seat Fokker EIII appeared in 1915. It had a machine gun that could fire through the **propeller arc** without hitting the blades. For months, the Fokker ruled the skies over northern France. This period was called the "Fokker Scourge" because the new planes were so deadly and effective.

World War II

By the start of World War II (1939–1945), fast, streamlined, all-metal monoplanes (planes with one set of wings) had replaced most of the biplanes. The new aircraft usually had covered cockpits and wheels that folded up. Machine guns and cannons were fitted into the wings. The new fighter's main task was to protect bombers as they attacked the enemy or to shoot down attacking enemy aircraft and their **fighter escorts.**

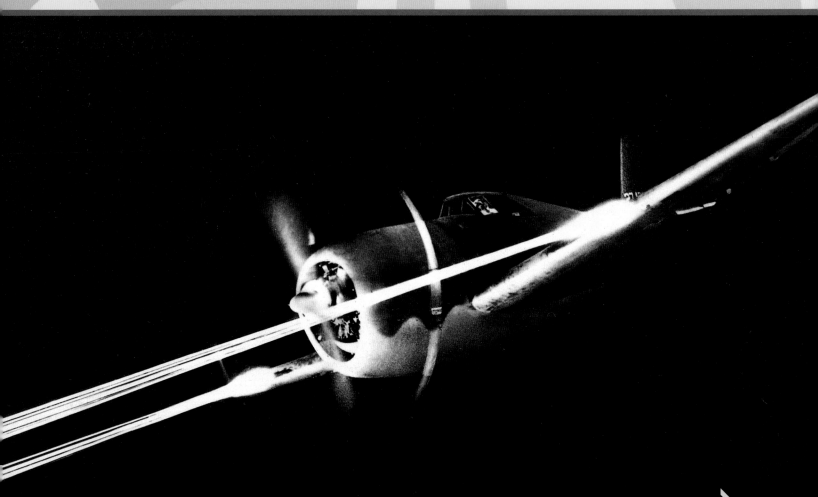

THUNDERBOLT

A U.S. P47 Thunderbolt fires its wing guns at night.

Escort Duty

TUSKEGEE AIRMEN

Veteran pilots of the 99th Fighter Squadron and the 332nd Fighter Group pose proudly in front of a restored B25 bomber. Known as the Tuskegee Airmen after their base in Alabama—or as the Red Tails because of their distinctive tailplane colouring—the squadron's members were all African Americans. Due to the policy of the time, they were not permitted to join white-only units. On combat escort duties in Europe, the Tuskegee Airmen had an impressive record. They flew 15,000 missions and downed 1,000 German aeroplanes, without losing a single bomber in their charge.

FRIENDS ABOVE

Vapour trails mark fighters escorting U.S. B17 Flying Fortress bombers over Germany. These fighters were usually P51 Mustangs, equipped with wing **drop tanks** that contained enough fuel to take them to the target and back home again.

The Fighter Role

A fighter's main job is to defend and protect. It keeps the skies free of enemy aircraft by striking them first. Many modern fighters are multi-role combat aircraft (MRCA), meaning that they can be used in both defensive and offensive roles.

FIRST JET FIGHTER

In the mid-1940s, Germany's twin-engine Me262 became the first working jet fighter. It could fly higher and faster and could climb more quickly than propeller-driven machines of the time. Although a great combat aeroplane, it came too late to change the outcome of World War II.

CHUCK YAEGER

In 1947 test pilot Chuck Yaeger became the first man to fly faster than the speed of sound. The first jet-on-jet combats occurred during the Korean War (1950–1953). American F86 Sabres tangled with Soviet-built planes over Communist-held North Korea.

TO SOUND AND BEYOND

Supersonic jet fighters are the most important part of a nation's air fleet, with many modern aircraft having multi-combat roles. This means they can be adapted for air-to-air combat, ground attack or bombing tasks.

FIGHTING FALCON

The Lockheed Martin F16 Fighting Falcon is a highly capable all-around fighter and bomber. It has **fly-by-wire** technology and Sidewinder air-to-air missiles on each wing.

DELTA DESIGN

A postwar U.S. Air Force Convair F106 Delta Dart. It was one of the world's first supersonic fighter aeroplanes.

Combat Air Patrol

In times of political or military tension, the Combat Air Patrol (CAP) is a first line of defense. Like an airborne police patrol, fighters keep watch against intruders. U.S. forces, as well as those of the North Atlantic Treaty Organization (NATO), have regularly flown CAPs in hotspots like Bosnia and the Persian Gulf to enforce United Nations (UN) **no-fly zones.**

EAGLE EYES

A U.S. F15 Eagle on CAP over Bosnia in 1996

Protecting the People

In the international war against air terror, fighter planes play a key role in protecting people and property against attacks. Operation Noble Eagle was mounted after the terror attacks of September 11, 2001, to safeguard U.S. citizens against air terror. A constant combat patrol keeps fighters in the skies 24 hours a day.

ALWAYS ON GUARD

Air National Guard F15s on patrol over New York City

Sight Unseen

The Lockheed-Martin F117 Nighthawk is a twin-engined, single-seat fighter with an attack role. First flown in 1981, the batlike Nighthawk remains at the front of combat aircraft technology. It is coated with a secret radar-absorbing material and is flown with the help of computerized controls. The Nighthawk can strike accurately at enemy defences without being found by radar. This means that most anti-aircraft weapons are unable to "see" it and therefore will not fire at it.

STEALTHY FIGHTER

The F117 uses **stealth** design to remain invisible to enemy guns and missiles. F117s flew many missions against Iraq and in Bosnia during the 1990s.

Fighters in Action

Nearly a century of aerial conflict separates the dogfights of World War I from modern long-distance, high-tech missile exchanges. Pilots and machines have changed but the basic goal remains the same: defending the skies from enemy intruders.

World War II

When the U.S. Army Air Force (USAAF) began sending bombers to Germany, the large, slow planes were easy targets for the fast German fighters. The U.S. bombers were shot down at an alarming rate. The P51D Mustang was introduced as a long-range escort fighter. It was able to follow and protect the bombers deep in enemy territory, saving the lives of many bomber crews. The U.S. **attrition rate** soon went down.

KEEPING WATCH

Long-range P51 Mustangs keep a lookout for enemy fighters as they escort a formation of USAAF B17 heavy bombers on a daylight raid over Germany in 1944.

MIGHTY MUSTANG

The North American P51 Mustang was an outstanding World War II fighter. It was originally built for the RAF. Early versions did not perform well at high altitudes, so the Mustang was refitted with a Rolls Royce Merlin engine. This combination resulted in the most successful fighter programme in history. Starting in 1941, more than 15,000 P51s were built, and many are still flying.

Details:
Crew: 1
Length: 33 ft.
Wingspan: 37 ft.
Propulsion: 1 x 1590 hp Merlin
Max Speed: 437 mph
Ceiling: 42,000 ft.
Armament: 6 x 0.5 in. Browning machine guns

MAKING HISTORY

"The Mustang was pleasant and forgiving to fly … We sensed it was special, even before we measured it against what the enemy pilots were flying."

Clarence "Bud" Anderson,
P51 fighter ace

"The day I saw Mustangs over Berlin, I knew the game was up."

Hermann Goering,
Hitler's deputy and commander in chief of the German air force

D DAY MUSTANG

A P51 Mustang in high-visibility **D day** stripes for easy identification.

Fighters in Action

The first jet fighter clashes took place during the Korean War. After Communist North Korea, with support from China, invaded South Korea, the United States and the UN responded. North American F86 Sabres fought against Soviet-built MiG15s for control of the skies over the Yalu River, an area that became known as "MiG Alley."

UN FORCES RETREAT

UN forces pull back across the **38th Parallel** following the Communist invasion in 1950.

SABRES RULE

An F86 Sabre. The MiG versus Sabre contests matched up the era's two best fighters. North Korea lost 792 MiGs to the loss of 78 Sabres. The air war was won and the Communists retreated.

>> **38th Parallel** – imaginary geographical line dividing North and South Korea

In 1981 tension between democratic nations and the Mediterranean nation of Libya were at their height. Libyan leader Muammar El-Qaddafi extended the country's territorial claim over the Mediterranean Sea from 2 to 12 miles, breaking international law. U.S. aircraft carriers sailed in to stop Libya from staking its claim.

Dogfight with Libya

TOMCAT REVENGE

A carrier-based Grumman F14 Tomcat

On August 19, 1981, two F14 Tomcats were flying a CAP in the skies near Libya in North Africa. Two Libyan Su22s approached and one fired its **Atoll** missile. The missile failed and the Tomcats attacked. The F14s shot down both SU22s using AIM9 Sidewinders. In 1989, in a similar incident, F14s took out two Libyan MiG23s.

Falklands War

In 1982 Argentine forces invaded the Falkland Islands off the Argentine coast. Argentina resented British ownership of the islands and its military government faced public unrest. Argentina's taking of the islands from the small Royal Marines unit gained popular support in Argentina. Britain responded by sending ships, planes and troops to the area. Argentine forces surrendered in July 1982.

HARRIER AT WAR

The Hawker Sea Harrier (the British version of the AV8 jump jet) was the only aircraft able to fly from the short decks of the Royal Navy's **VSTOL** carriers. RAF and Royal Navy pilots flew a total of 1,435 missions against Argentine targets during the two-month conflict. They shot down at least 20 planes, with no losses of their own.

Desert Storm

During the 1991 Persian Gulf War against Iraq, U.S. and **Coalition** fighter forces flew a number of missions. The 58th Fighter Squadron, part of the 33rd Fighter Wing based at Eglin Air Force Base, Florida, was one of the units that served with success.

FAR FROM HOME

A 58th Tactical Fighter Squadron F15 Eagle over the Iraqi desert in 1991.

RISKY BUSINESS

"There are pilots and there are pilots; with the good ones, it is inborn. You can't teach it. If you are a fighter pilot, you have to be willing to take risks."

General Robin Olds, U.S. Air Force

MIG DOWN

An Iraqi pilot ejects from his destroyed MiG. On January 17, 1991, Captain John Kelk scored the first air-to-air victory by shooting down a Russian-built Iraqi MiG29. The 58th Fighter Squadron destroyed five MiG29s, more any other squadron during the five-week air war.

Fighter Tactics

A fighter plane is only as good as the pilot who flies it. The pilot relies on training and proven methods of attack. Nearly a century of air warfare has produced fighting tactics that in some cases go back to World War I.

Golden Rules

Attack from above and behind; watch for attackers against the sun; keep searching the sky. All these basic air combat laws date back to World War I, when aviation created a new kind of warfare.

KNOW WHERE YOU ARE

A fighter pilot must keep continuous lookout and not be confused by making high-speed moves.

>> **flying circus** = a World War I term for a large group of aeroplanes

FORMATIONS

F16 Flying Falcons in a tight V formation. Most formations are made up of combinations of aircraft in twos or threes. The pilots on the leader's wings keep a defensive watch, while the leader seeks out the enemy. Other formations include finger four, line abreast and line astern.

SAFETY IN NUMBERS

Large **flying circuses** and "wings" were a feature of both world wars. Dozens of aeroplanes, all flying in **formation,** were a powerful anti-enemy force. The downside was the length of time it sometimes took to gather so many machines at a time.

EYES ALL AROUND

In the finger four formation, adopted in World War II, a section of four aircraft each guards a portion of the sky.

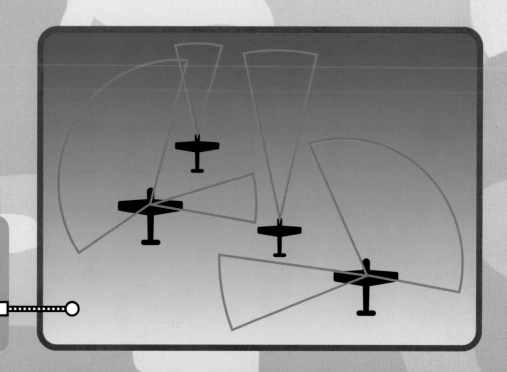

Fighter Tactics

In modern warfare, the aeroplane that has the tightest turning circle (the diameter of a 360 degree turn) has an advantage. It can always turn out of an attacker's line of fire. With precision-guided missile technology, the turn is less important. But ease of movement can still outsmart a missile.

HARRIER JUMP JET

The jump jet can perform manoeuvres that no other type of fighter can match. It uses its **vectored thrust nozzles** to skip out of its flight path. This tactic is known as "viffing," for vectoring-in-flight. This Harrier (*top*) is thrusting away from its Sepecat Jaguar wingman.

ELECTRONIC WARFARE

Most modern air-to-air contacts rely on technology to identify and strike a target. The enemy may be beyond visual range but can be targeted by radar. Precision guided "fire and forget" missiles can then **lock-on**, travelling at speeds of Mach 4 (four times the speed of sound, about 2500 mph).

> vecto   off

A Navy F/A18 Hornet crashes through the sound barrier in a burst of vapour. The greatest advantage any fighter plane has is its speed, both in attack and in defence.

ALWAYS TRUE

"The most important thing to a fighter pilot is speed. The faster an aircraft is moving when he spots the enemy, the sooner he will be able to take the bounce .... It's like sneaking up behind someone with a baseball bat."

Duane W. Beeson, P51 Mustang pilot, 1945

Fighters

Fighter aircraft are the first defence against enemy airborne attack. The planes are fast and comparatively small. Just one or sometimes two pilots make up the crew. Fighters and those who fly them are the best of the best in the air.

F16 FIGHTING FALCON

The Lockheed Martin F16 Fighting Falcon was introduced as a smaller and cheaper version of the F15 Eagle. It has since performed well as both a fighter and a fighter-bomber in combat and in advanced training roles.

Details:
Crew: 1
Length: 30 ft.
Wingspan: 47 ft. 7 in.
Propulsion: 1 x 24,000 lb. thrust **turbofan**
Max Speed: 1,300 mph
Ceiling: 60,000 ft.
Armament: 1 x 20mm cannon, 15,200 lb. **external load**

F15 EAGLE

The McDonnell Douglas F15 is a fighter specifically developed to meet the threat thought to come from the Soviet Union's MiG23s and MiG25s. There is a dual-seat advanced-trainer version (*shown*) and a single-seat combat model.

Details:
Crew: 1–2
Length: 63 ft.
Wingspan: 42 ft. 9 in.
Propulsion: 2 x 23,800 lb. thrust turbofan
Max Speed: 1,650 mph
Ceiling: 70,000 ft.
Armament: 1 x 20mm cannon, 12,000 lb. external load

F4 PHANTOM

The McDonnell Douglas F4 is one of the world's all-time great combat aircraft. Rugged and adaptable, it has seen active service with air forces across the world for several decades. As a land-based fighter-bomber and carrier-based fighter, it has an outstanding record.

Details:
Crew: 2
Length: 58 ft. 3 in.
Wingspan: 38 ft. 5 in. (spread)
Propulsion: 2 x 20,515 lb. thrust afterburning turbofans
Max Speed: 1,500 mph
Ceiling: 60,000 ft.
Armament: 1 x 20mm cannon, 16,000 lb. external load

Fighters

SU27 "FLANKER"

Dubbed "Flanker" by NATO, the Sukhoi 27 is a Russian-built **air-superiority fighter** like the F15 Eagle. There is a carrier-based version, the Su33, and a two-seat, side-by-side strike model, the Su34.

Details:
Crew: 1
Length: 71 ft. 9 in.
Wingspan: 48 ft.
Propulsion: 2 x 27,557 lb. thrust afterburning turbofan
Max Speed: 1,555 mph at altitude
Ceiling: 59,000 ft.
Armament: 1 x 30mm cannon, bombs, and air-to-air missiles

MIG29 "FULCRUM"

The MiG29 "Fulcrum" is a Russian-built all-weather fighter and strike aeroplane that can carry **nuclear warheads**. It has a helmet-mounted line-of-sight weapon system that steers its missiles where the pilot looks. It compares with the F/A18 and the F15.

Details:
Crew: 1
Length: 56 ft. 10 in.
Wingspan: 36 ft. 5 in.
Propulsion: 2 x 22,200 lb. thrust turbofan
Max Speed: 1,520 mph
Ceiling: 60,000 ft.
Armament: 1 x 30mm cannons, variable missile load

>> **air-superiority fighter** = an aeroplane designed to knock out any opposition

SU37 "TERMINATOR"

The all-weather Sukhoi 37 is easy to fly and is the multi-role fighter version of the Su27. It is Russia's most advanced fighting aeroplane. It has fully digitized fly-by-wire controls.

Details:
Crew: 1
Length: 72 ft.
Wingspan: 49 ft. 9 in.
Propulsion: 2 x 30,855 lb. vectored-thrust afterburning turbofans
Max Speed: 1,516 mph
Ceiling: 59,000 ft.
Armament: 1 x 30mm cannon, 18,075 lb. bomb and/or missile load

Fighters

MIRAGE 2000

The Dassault-Breguet Mirage 2000 is a combat-proven fighter-interceptor built in France. The Mirage delta-wing fighter, one of the most technically advanced combat aircraft in the world, is in service with air forces in many countries.

Details:
Crew: 1
Length: 50 ft. 3 in.
Wingspan: 29 ft. 5 in.
Propulsion: 1 x 15,873 lb. thrust afterburning turbofan
Max Speed: 1,450 mph
Ceiling: 50,000 ft.
Armament: 2 x 30mm cannons, 8,820 lb. ordnance load

SEPECAT JAGUAR

The Jaguar is a joint French and British fighter-bomber. The fighter version is equipped with twin cannons and **ASRAAM** (short-range air-to-air missiles). The strike version is in use with several other countries, including India and Oman and can be adapted to carry nuclear weapons.

Details:
Crew: 1
Length: 55 ft. 2 in.
Wingspan: 28 ft. 6 in.
Propulsion: 2 x 7305 lb. thrust afterburning
   turbofans
Max Speed: 900 mph
Ceiling: 40,000 ft.
Armament: 1 x 30mm Arden cannon,
   10,000 lb. **ordnance** load

JAS39 GRIPEN

The JAS39 Gripen (Griffin) is built by Saab Military Industries, a Swedish world leader in combat aircraft design. The Gripen is a compact multi-role fighter with air defence and strike capabilities.

Details:
Crew: 1
Length: 46 ft. 3 in.
Wingspan: 27 ft. 7 in.
Propulsion: 1 x 18,100 lb. thrust afterburning
   turbofan
Max Speed: 1,321 mph
Ceiling: 50,000 ft.
Armament: 1 x 27mm Mauser cannon,
   14,330 lb. bomb and missile load

Fighters

A7 CORSAIR II

The Vought Corsair II was one of the longest-serving carrier-based aircraft flown by the U.S. Navy. Corsairs saw action in Vietnam in the 1960s and against Libyan terrorist targets in the 1980s. After two decades of service, the aeroplane was replaced by the F/A18 Hornet.

Details:
Crew: 1
Length: 46 ft.
Wingspan: 38 ft. 9 in.
Propulsion: 1 x 11,350 lb. thrust turbofans
Max Speed: 645 mph at patrol level
Ceiling: 35,000 ft.
Armament: 1 x 20mm cannon, 20,000 lb. ordnance load

F14 TOMCAT

The Grumman F14 Tomcat is a supersonic all-weather interceptor with **variable geometry wings.** It is the U.S. Navy's most advanced fighter plane and can track up to 24 aircraft at one time. The F14 was designed as a replacement for the F4 Phantom.

Details:
Crew: 2
Length: 61 ft. 9 in.
Wingspan: 64 ft. unswept
Propulsion: 2 x 20,900 lb. thrust afterburning turbofans
Max Speed: 1,564 mph
Ceiling: 53,000 ft.
Armament: 1 x 20mm cannon, 14,500 lb. bomb and missile load

F5 TIGER II

The Northrop F5 is a small fighter and advanced trainer that has a history dating back to the 1950s. Lightweight and reliable, its flight advantages (similar to the Russian MiG21) have led to its adoption as an enemy aircraft simulator for combat training.

Details:
Crew: 1
Length: 48 ft. 2 in.
Wingspan: 26 ft. 8 in.
Propulsion: 2 x 5000 lb. thrust afterburning **turbojets**
Max Speed: 640 mph at sea level
Ceiling: 51,800 ft.
Armament: 2 x 20mm cannons, 5000 lb. ordnance load

Fighters of the Future

The next generation of combat aircraft will be faster, easier to move around and better equipped than current frontline fighters. The emphasis will be on stealth and on more accurate and harder-hitting missile systems.

ENTER THE RAPTOR

The F22 Raptor, developed by Boeing and Lockheed Martin, is set to replace the F15 Eagle air-superiority fighter. It will become operational with U.S. and allied air forces and navies during the first decade of the twenty-first century. The F22 will combine stealth design with supersonic ease of movement. Its state-of-the-art target-finding and missile delivery systems will make the Raptor the world leader for many years.

X-Planes Explained

X31 ENHANCED MANOEUVRABILIY DEMONSTRATOR

The X31 tests thrust-vectoring techniques. Many aeroplanes are developed just to try out different **airframes** or technology and never go to full-scale manufacture. In the United States, these are known as X-Planes and are tested in great secrecy at places like the famous Lockheed Martin "Skunk Works" at Edwards Air Force Base in California. Stealth and variable geometry are two examples of the technology resulting from these trials. These tests give U.S. manufacturers a cutting edge in future fighter production.

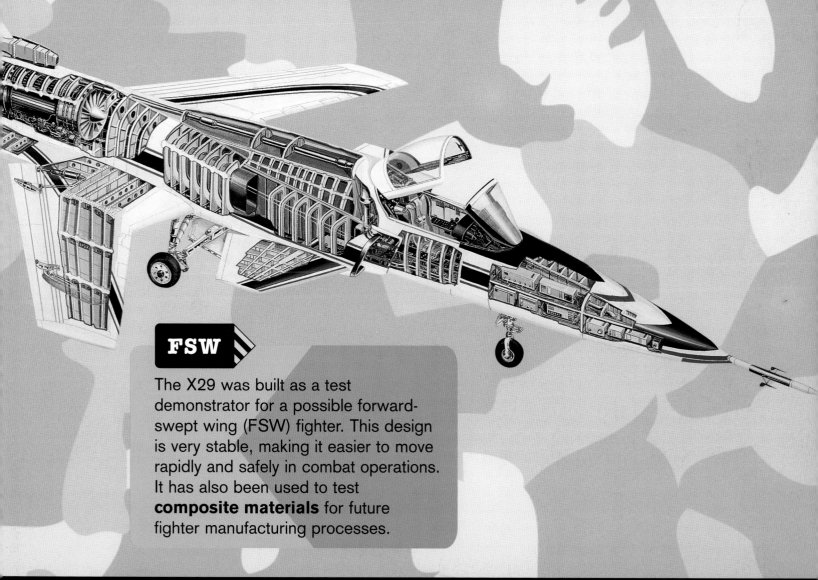

FSW

The X29 was built as a test demonstrator for a possible forward-swept wing (FSW) fighter. This design is very stable, making it easier to move rapidly and safely in combat operations. It has also been used to test **composite materials** for future fighter manufacturing processes.

Index

Picture Sources